This book is dedicated to my sweet patients and the families
I have had the honor of caring for in hospice.

To my loving family for supporting me throughout this journey.
To 'Papa' who inspired the writing behind this book. His heart of gold and love for
his family will always be memorable. To his beautiful grandchildren, who will carry his
legacy and will do amazing things in this world. To Gammie, who cared for 'Papa'.
Never leaving his side, she was always his biggest advocate and greatest support.
It was an absolute honor to care for 'Papa' and his family.

Most of all, this book is dedicated to God, the One who gave me the words to write.
May God get all of the glory for this book!

Names: McCrary, Jordan, author. | Swift, Amanda, 1984- illustrator.
Title: Heaven's waiting room / written by Jordan McCrary ; art by Amanda Swift.
Description: [Freeport, Florida] : [Jordan McCrary], [2025] | Summary: "Heaven's Waiting Room" is a faith-filled children's book, written by a hospice nurse, that gently helps children understand the changes when a loved one enters hospice care. A special kind of care focused on comfort, love, and peace at the end of life.—Publisher.
Identifiers: LCCN: 2025915606 | ISBN: 9798999595447 (hardcover) | 9798999595478 (paperback) | 9798999595423 (eBook)
Subjects: LCSH: Hospice care—Juvenile fiction. | Terminal care—Religious aspects—Juvenile fiction. | Terminally ill—Juvenile fiction. | Heaven—Juvenile fiction. | Death—Religious aspects—Juvenile fiction. | CYAC: Hospices (Terminal care)—Fiction. | Terminally ill—Fiction. | Heaven—Fiction. | Death—Religious aspects—Fiction.
Classification: LCC: PZ7.1.M432 H43 2025 | DDC: [Fic]—dc23

Heaven's
WAITING ROOM

written by
Jordan McCrary

art by
Amanda Swift

"Papa, do you want to go play today?"

"That sounds like fun. I can go right after my doctor's appointment."

Hi!

"Papa, you look sad."

"Ice cream always makes me feel better.
I'm glad we went out for some!"

"Papa, who is this?"

"This is my hospice nurse, Ann. She comes to my home twice a week to take care of me. She has to listen to my heart, my lungs, and my tummy. Then she tells my doctor how I'm doing."

"Papa, do you want to go for a walk?"

"If you can keep up!"

"Papa, do you want to go fishing?"

"Let's go."

"Papa, what do you want to do today?"

"Let's have a movie day."

"Papa, why do you look so tired?"

"The nurse says I have my good days
and bad days. Come sit with me.
You can pick the movie."

"Papa, Keep up!"

"Papa, what is that?"

"This is my new ride."

"Papa, what is that machine for?"

"It's to help my lungs breathe.
Come take a closer look.
I promise it's not scary."

"Papa, why did you get a new bed?"

"It's more comfortable and will
move up and down if I need it to.
Do you want to ride up and down?"

"Papa, can we order pizza?"

"I don't get that hungry anymore,
but we can get some for you!"

"Papa, why does Nurse Ann come and see you more now?"

"It's her job to check on me and make sure I'm comfortable."

"Papa, what is Nurse Ann doing?"

"She's listening to my heart. Do you want to hear it?"

ba-dum
ba-dum
ba-dum

"Papa, what is hospice?"

"Hospice means that a big team of special people visit me at home to make sure I'm comfortable, and that I'm able to enjoy spending time with you for as long as I can! Does that make sense?"

"I think so."

"Here, come sit with me. Do you know what Heaven is?"

"No."

"It's a beautiful place, with streets of gold and a man named Jesus. Soon, Jesus will come and take me home to Heaven."

"Papa, I don't want you to leave me."

"It's okay to be sad. I will always be with you. Right there in your heart."

"Papa, can I go to Heaven?"

"One day, when the time is right, you can go.
But it's not time for you yet."

"Papa, I love you."

"I love you more."

"Did Papa go to heaven?"

"Yes, he did."

I am a hospice nurse, and I believe in the power of prayer.
It would be considered an honor to pray over you
and your loved one.

Dear God,

I want to thank whoever is reading this prayer. I want to thank You for their life. God, things don't feel good right now. But God, You are good, Lord. I lift up this family and their loved one right now. You made the promise in Psalm 34 that You are near to the broken-hearted. So, Lord, I ask You to be near to this family right now—near to these children and whoever is reading this.

God, You are the Great Physician, and your timing is perfect. Take away all pain or discomfort. I ask You to bring an overwhelming peace into this home and surpass all understanding. Allow the right people and hands to work with this loved one. Jesus, I want to thank you for dying on the cross for our sins. Thank you for the gift of salvation. If there is any doubt right now, Lord, I ask You to make this the moment that they truly surrender their life to You—that they may find everlasting joy.

Jesus, I know you love this family. I ask you to hold them tight during this difficult time and make your presence known. May the Lord bless you and shine His face upon you during this difficult time.
In Jesus' name I pray.

Amen.

www.ingramcontent.com/pod-product-compliance
Lightning Source LLC
Chambersburg PA
CBHW041559120626
46551CB00002B/262